WHAT IS A SNOWBOARDER?

What is a snowboarder? It's a tough question to answer. Most snowboarders are young, but sometimes you see 60-year-olds having their first lesson. Almost as many girls take up the sport as boys.

'Surf interdit': no snowboarding.

Ban This Evil Craze!

When snowboarding first appeared, some ski resorts tried to ban it. It was seen as unsafe, with out-of-control riders posing a danger to the skiing traffic. Many riders were forced to ride off-piste, away from the authorities.

Even now, when snowboarders are allowed to ride the whole mountain, many riders say off-piste or freeriding is the sport's purest form.

SNOWBOARDING

Paul Mason

An imprint of Hodder Children's Books

to the limit
SNOWBOARDING

Other titles in this well-cool series are:

BLADING
MOTOCROSS
MOUNTAINBIKING
SKATEBOARDING
SURFING

Prepared for Hodder Wayland by Roger Coote Publishing, Gissings Farm, Fressingfield, Eye, Suffolk IP21 5SH

© Hodder Wayland 2000

Project Management: Mason Editorial Services
Designer: Tim Mayer

Published in 2001 by
Hodder Wayland, an imprint of
Hodder Children's Books

A Catalogue record for this book is available from the British Library.

ISBN 0 7502 2787 7

Printed and bound in Italy by G. Canale & C. S.p.A., Turin

Hodder Children's Books
A division of Hodder Headline limited
338 Euston Road, London NW1 3BH

WARNING!
Snowboarding is a dangerous sport. This book is full of advice, but reading it won't keep you safe on the mountain. Take responsibility for your own safety, and get lessons.

The Secret Language Of Snowboarding

Binding: The link between your feet and the board.

Deck: The snowboard itself.

Fakie: Backwards (as in a goofy-foot rider with his or her left foot downhill).

Goofy foot: A boarder who rides with his or her right foot forwards.

half-pipe: A chute with steeply banked sides, used for performing jumps.

Planker: Skier (refers to skiers having planks on their feet).

Regular foot: A boarder who rides with her or his left foot forwards.

The Early Days

In the Sixties people tried to mate surfing and skateboarding with snow. Early attempts were. . . unsafe, to say the least. It was assumed you'd need to be able to jump off if things got hairy. We now know, of course, that if you can control your board by being attached to it, things are less likely to go wrong.

An inventor from the East Coast of the USA, Jake Burton, was the first to come up with something we'd recognise as an early snowboard. Most early boards were ridden more or less straight downhill, which may account for snowboarding having been banned in some places. . . but they worked.

The rest is history.

Left: an early snowboard. Below: someone having a lot of fun on one.

Jake Burton

Although he's still a young man, Jake Burton could reasonably be called the Grandfather of Snowboarding. The company he founded from his garage is now a multi-million dollar business employing hundreds of people, with branches all round the world.

Jake may be the grandfather of snowboarding, but he still rips!

Early Fashions

Early on the only things that kept you warm enough to go out riding were ski clothes. The snow fashions of the time included neon one-piece suits and bright-pink fluffy headbands. Enough said. . .

EQUIPMENT

There are an amazing number of different types of equipment for snowboarding; some of them even do what the makers claim. Despite what the ads suggest, though, no one has yet invented snowboarding equipment that makes you attractive to the opposite sex.

Wide nose allows the board to rise through powder snow.

Set-back stance for directional riding.

Step-in bindings are easier and quicker to use.

More sidecut gives a longer turning edge and more grip.

Stiffer tail gives snappy turns and set-back riding position.

Freeride board and bindings

Freeride:

For riding off-piste and in powder, boards tend to be longer and single-directional, although you can ride them fakie if required.

Stiffer boots transfer movement to the board more quickly

8

Shorter length gives lighter weight: easier to jump and twist.

Flexible tail better for landing jumps.

Kit for snowboarding boils down to three essentials: the board, the boots, and the bindings. Various types of each of these has been developed to suit particular riding styles: freeride, freestyle/half-pipe or piste racing. But most boards are able to do everything, even if they ride better in one style than the others.

Centred stance for easy fakie riding.

Strap bindings allow the board to move more freely during tricks and jumps.

Less sidecut makes the board feel 'looser' and more slidey.

Freestyle/ half-pipe board and bindings:

Less rigid boots give a 'looser' feel and more flexible response.

These boards are shorter, lighter and symmetrical (the same shape at both ends) because they have to be ridden fakie after airs and spins have been landed.

Clothing and stuff

Here's a secret. It's the single thing that will make you a better boarder, learn tricks more quickly, and ride faster for longer. A special pill? Hypnosis? A particular make of board? None of the above – the best thing you can do on a mountain is to stay warm.

Ready-to-ride checklist

- ☑ Hat (not wool)
- ☑ Goggles
- ☑ Thermal top
- ☑ Fleece
- ☑ Gloves – must be for snowboarding
- ☑ Thermal bottoms – often not needed
- ☑ Water bottle
- ☑ Small rucksack (for storing clothes)
- ☑ Snowboard tool
- ☑ Emergency money
- ☑ Spare thermal top
- ☑ Scarf (not wool)

Snowboarding pants

- Waterproof, reinforced seat for sitting on cold snow.
- Seals at bottom stop snow entry.
- Some pants have side vents to cool down hot legs.
- Fleece panel at back mops up sweat.
- Some pants have pockets.

If you're not warm, your body slows down. Your brain demands that heat from the rest of your body is concentrated in your head and around your heart: you move more slowly, you don't have as much energy and your co-ordination disappears. If you get really cold, you stop thinking clearly. If you stay cold enough for long enough, you die.

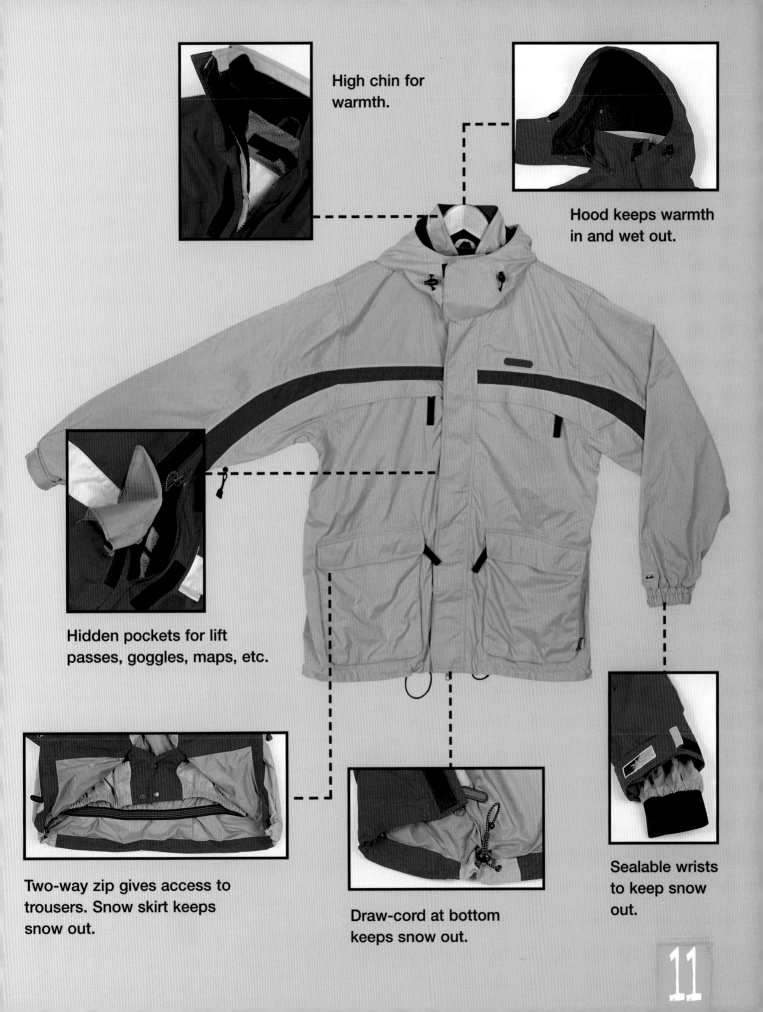

High chin for warmth.

Hood keeps warmth in and wet out.

Hidden pockets for lift passes, goggles, maps, etc.

Two-way zip gives access to trousers. Snow skirt keeps snow out.

Draw-cord at bottom keeps snow out.

Sealable wrists to keep snow out.

BASICS

Although snowboarding can be quite hard to learn, there are really only two basic techniques:

- the frontside turn (where you turn on your toe edge, facing into the turn);
- the heelside turn (where you turn on your heel, with your back to the turn).

Once you can do each of these, as long as you take care you should be able to ride on almost any piste, as well as doing easy off-piste runs through powder.

Heelside turn

1 Keep your body relaxed and your centre of gravity low, with your knees bent.

2 Start to turn your hips round in the direction you want to turn. At the same time put your weight gently through your thighs and into your heels.

3 As you come into the line you want, ease off the pressure until you're travelling straight.

Frontside turn

Keep your body relaxed and your centre of gravity low, with your knees bent.

5, 6, 7 Turn your hips slightly in the direction you want to go, and put your weight gently through your hips and into your toes/the pads of your feet. Keep your weight more or less even between your front and back foot.

8, 9 As you come into the line you want, ease the pressure off the toe edge until the board is travelling straight.

FEAR WARNING!

Snowboards are always ridden on one of their two edges. The only time this is not true is during a turn or when riding in powder. As you turn from one edge to the other, there's a moment when the board is flat on the ground. It can accelerate very quickly: to stop this happening you must continue the turn and get back on an edge. COMMITMENT IS EVERYTHING!

STYLE WARNING!

Snatched turns, where the board flicks round and scrapes the snow, are not good style. Aim for a smooth turn done without too much sliding.

Powder

Most snowboarders start to learn with a particular kind of riding in mind. Some want to become a demon in the fun parks and half-pipes; others imagine themselves riding off-piste having been dropped by helicopter at the top of a remote peak.

Powder technique

Riding through powder demands much more power in your back foot. This is because your front foot is being used to keep the nose of the board from sinking down and burying in the snow. It feels a bit like doing a wheelie, lifting the front of the deck to keep it moving.

To ride the whole mountain you need to be able to ride through powder snow. This almost always means snowboarding off-piste, which can be extremely dangerous. Not 'you-might-scrape-your-knee-or-bang-your-arm' kind of dangerous, but 'you-might-end-up-dead' kind of dangerous. NEVER ride off-piste powder runs without a qualified guide.

Anthony Gumbly: massive frontside turn in Val d'Isere, France.

Stay safe

Every year a lot of people are killed riding off-piste. Never go off-piste without an experienced local guide. It might look fun, but is it worth dying for?

Never follow another rider's tracks: they might be far better than you, or they might be lying dead at the bottom of a cliff just around the next turn. Just because someone else did it, doesn't make it safe for you.

James Stentiford makes the most of a big bank of powder.

Freeride

For many people, this is the heart of what snowboarding is really about. Freeriding is just what the word suggests: riding where you want, how you like. Off-piste, on-piste, through trees, on an open mountainside, with jumps, without jumps: whatever you choose, you're freeriding. The only rule is, there are no rules except to keep yourself safe and not endanger others.

Chamonix, France

'The lift system,' says *The World Snowboard Guide 3* of Chamonix, 'gives you access to so much off-piste that you'd never get to see all of it in a million seasons.'

Chamonix is the capital of mountain sports in Europe, and one of the best places anywhere to go freeriding (or to watch extreme riders from a safe place!). Beware, though: 'bail in this place and you may not live to regret it.'

Jonny Barr enjoys some of the finest conditions in Chamonix, France.

Freeride checklist:

- ☑ **Warm clothes (see page 10-11)**
- ☑ **Avalanche beeper (helps searchers find you if you're buried)**
- ☑ **Avalanche probe (helps you find buried people)**
- ☑ **Folding spade**
- ☑ **Survival bag**
- ☑ **Food: chocolate for energy boost, cheese for slow-burn warmth**
- ☑ **Mobile phone**

Advanced riders only need apply!

Heli-boarding

Expert riders flock to Canada and Alaska each winter to go heli-boarding. A helicopter picks them up from a snowboard camp and drops them off at the top of a mountain. The only way down is to ride.

Arguably the U.S.A.'s steepest freeride resort: Jackson Hole, Wyoming.

17

Ollies

For every boarder who swears freeriding is what snowboarding is all about, another will tut and say 'No way, man: you need to get some air.' He or she doesn't mean you need to go for a healthy walk: this is all about getting airborne.

The style of riding that focuses on jumps, spins, slides and tricks is sometimes called freestyle. In freestyle, riders line themselves up on a kicker and practise a particular move again and again, until they've got it right or they're in hospital. This kind of snowboarding borrows heavily from skateboarding: lots of the jumps use the same names (though not always to describe the same move) and the clothes and attitude are shared.

1 Centre your weight.

2 Lift up the nose.

3 Pull the tail up.

4 Relax.

Ollie technique

The rule with this is to start small and build up the size. Even the best riders do this when they're learning a new technique. To ollie, you lift the front foot up into the air, then leap the back foot up behind it. Sounds impossible and feels impossible when you first try, but it comes with practice.

5 Ride away with a big smile!

METHOD AIR – Simon Brass

FRONTSIDE 360 TAILGRAB – Elliot Neave

FRONTSIDE 540 stalefish – Stu Brass

19

Half-pipe heaven

Somewhere in every mountain resort that takes itself seriously you'll find a half-pipe. Probably it will be filled with bruised boarders, trudging back to the top for just one more go. Half-pipe boarders go back and forth between two jumps, performing twists and airs on each. When it goes right this is very spectacular: when it goes wrong it can be very painful. And it tends to go wrong a lot more than it goes right.

Terje Haakonsen: McTwist tailbone at the U.S. Open Championships, Stratton, Vermont.

A rider slides his way to half-pipe heaven.

Summer Camp (with a twist)

Snowboard summer camps are set up all over the world on glaciers. The boarders dig out half-pipes, camp down in the valley and hike or drive up every day for the two hours when the snow's in condition, between rock-hard ice (morning) and sun-drenched slush (afternoon).

There are alternatives: in quarter-pipe, riders line up on just one jump, which they approach at high speed, aiming to go as high as they can. The trouble with this is that you can do even more damage than you can on a half-pipe.

If these opportunities to bang yourself up aren't enough, there are jumps of all sizes on and around pistes in snowboarding areas. Most of these are built by boarders, but some occur naturally and others are just there – sloping roofs, benches and fallen trees can all be used for logging airtime.

Can you make a living?

For many riders, the ultimate dream would be to be paid to be a snowboarder. It sounds glamorous: travelling round the world for competitions, being flown to fantastic places by your sponsor to shoot a video or an advertising campaign. Some of the top riders were recently paid to shoot video sequences that were used in Playstation's 'Snowboarding' game.

Nicola Thost at a night-time half-pipe competition at Salen, Sweden.

Girls? Girls!

There are some excellent female pro riders. Snowboarding has always been popular with girls – in many European resorts there as many women riding as men. Snowboarders like Cara-Beth Burnside (also an excellent skateboarder) and Nicola Thost continue to show that female riders are able to pull off spectacular moves, just as well as the boys.

The reality of being a pro (or semi-pro) snowboarder is very different for most people. Most sponsorship deals are for equipment or clothing: you have to pay for travelling to competitions and living expenses yourself. Which means getting a job that allows you time off for snowboarding. . . which means working as a waiter or stacking shelves in a supermarket. . . which isn't so much fun.

Even so some people do make it, and once you're sponsored by a major company life is sweet. The important thing to remember is not to kid yourself about how good you are: it's only supernaturally good riders that get even minor sponsorship deals.

**The rewards of sponsorship:
helicopters + snowmobiles = fun.**

An artificial-snow competition.

The scales of sponsorship

Level 1 – You persuade a local shop to sell you reduced-price equipment. You'd need to have come in the top three of some competitions.

Level 2 – The local shop starts giving you equipment.

Level 3 – A representative from a big company approaches you. Now they'll give you stuff, and maybe even some money. You need to be a national-standard rider.

Level 4 – Big time: the big company wants you to ride for them full time. For this, you'd have to be one of the world's best boarders.

23

COMPETITION

Snowboarding started as an underground activity with an 'us against the rest' attitude, so competitions were friendly get-togethers where people showed off their new tricks. Today, competitions are contests, but they're conducted in a friendly, hassle-free way that people from most other sports wouldn't recognise.

As more and more money creeps into snowboarding things get less and less friendly. Still, winning or losing depends on your own performance, not someone else's, so the emphasis is on what you can do rather than beating other people.

Floodlit night-time competitions are increasingly popular.

Competition formats

Half-pipe Competitors take it in turns to ride down the half-pipe and are scored by judges on the moves they make.

Slalom A bit like skiing slalom, weaving between poles trying to get down fastest. In snowboarding two riders race side-by-side, and the winner advances to the next round.

Aerial Competitions such as the Innsbruck Air and Style fix huge ramps off which the riders jump in an effort to impress the judges.

Extreme Terrifying: riders take it in turns to see who can get down a whole mountain in the quickest time by the hardest route. Death wish required to enter...

STR TTON
Vermont's Mountain Resort

25

MOUNTAIN SAFETY

Crash!. . .

. . . Bang!. . .

Most mountain resorts are a form of organized mayhem. Sometimes there are thousands of people out on the slopes, all with varying levels of ability and most going very fast.

In an effort to avoid collisions, people have invented a few simple rules that everyone should follow while out snowboarding.
At some resorts you risk being thrown off the mountain and told not to come back if you don't follow these. This is very upsetting, especially if you have five days of a six-day pass in your pocket.

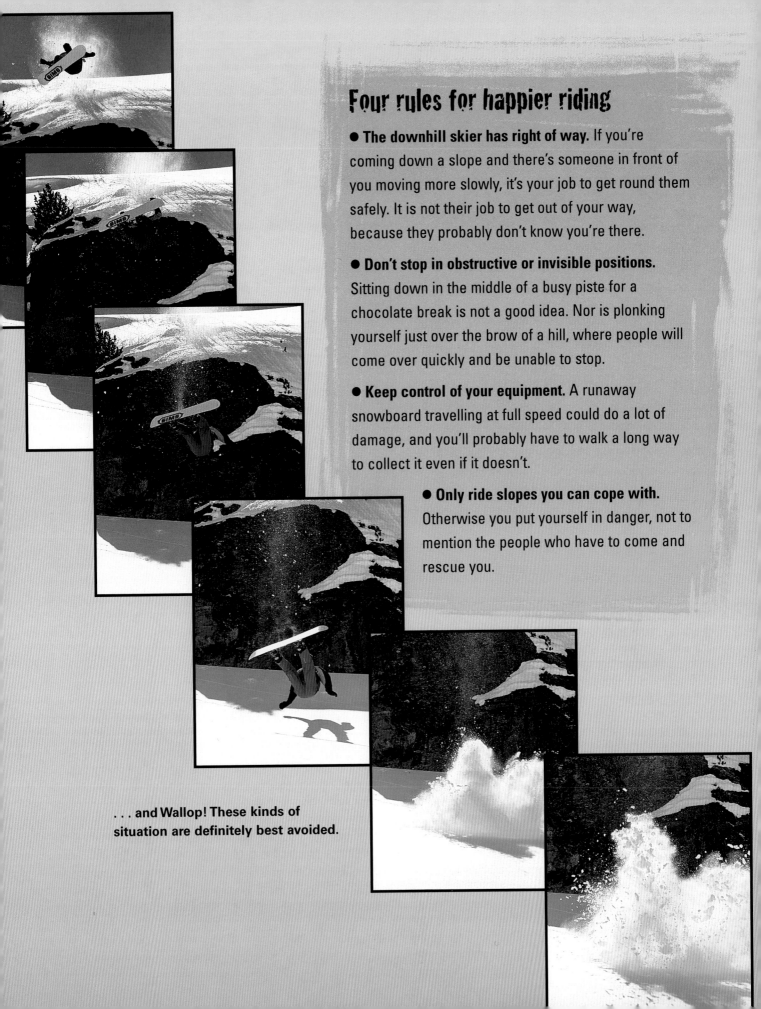

Four rules for happier riding

● **The downhill skier has right of way.** If you're coming down a slope and there's someone in front of you moving more slowly, it's your job to get round them safely. It is not their job to get out of your way, because they probably don't know you're there.

● **Don't stop in obstructive or invisible positions.** Sitting down in the middle of a busy piste for a chocolate break is not a good idea. Nor is plonking yourself just over the brow of a hill, where people will come over quickly and be unable to stop.

● **Keep control of your equipment.** A runaway snowboard travelling at full speed could do a lot of damage, and you'll probably have to walk a long way to collect it even if it doesn't.

● **Only ride slopes you can cope with.** Otherwise you put yourself in danger, not to mention the people who have to come and rescue you.

. . . and Wallop! These kinds of situation are definitely best avoided.

Have you been paying attention?

That's right: there's a quiz at the end of the book. This one is designed not only to see whether you're a fit person to go snowboarding, but also to analyse your character. Not really: it's just about snowboarding.

1 You're leaning your board against the railing of a mountain café. A skier goes past very close to you, just after someone shouts 'Planker!' Do you say:

a) 'Where? And why would anyone be carrying planks around up here? Don't be so silly.'
b) 'Who are you calling a planker?'
c) 'Thanks for the warning. He was pretty close, wasn't he?'

2 Is Burton:

a) A famous explorer or film actor?
b) The word button, but said in a strange way?
c) The Grandfather of Snowboarding?

3 Shorter decks are better for freestyle riders because:

a) They make you look taller.
b) They fit in the cable car more easily.
c) They're lighter and easier to spin.

4 Step-in bindings are popular because:

a) They're quicker to get into and out of.
b) You don't have to spend ages sitting on cold snow putting your bindings on.
c) Both of the above.

5 The most important thing about your clothing is:

a) That it's in this year's colours, and has the right labels on it.
b) That it all goes well together, and matches your hair, too. Lovely!
c) That it keeps you warm and dry.

6 The best place to sit down for a rest is:

a) The middle of the piste: there's a lovely view, and you can watch everyone go by.
b) Below a crest on the slope: it keeps the wind off.
c) The edge of the piste: everyone can see you, and you're out of the way.

7 Your way is blocked by a slow-moving beginner. Do you:

a) Shout 'Oi! Get off the road, slowcoach!'
b) Aim for a narrow gap and hope he or she doesn't turn.
c) Slow down to the same speed and wait for the piste to widen enough to get through safely.

How did you do?

Mostly a) Are you the kind of person who reads books from the back forwards? You just looked at the pictures, didn't you?

Mostly b) You just looked at the pictures and read the captions, right?

Mostly c) You have done well. Next time you go snowboarding, can I come?

28

Glossary

Word:	Means:	Dosen't Mean:
Binding	The link between your feet and the board.	Rope for tying up your enemies.
Chutes	Narrow tracks down the side of a mountain, usually with steep rocks above each side.	Fires a gun.
Deck	The snowboard itself.	Top of a ship.
Edge	The thin metal edge of the board, which bites into the snow. Also sometimes called a rail.	Creep along.
Fakie	Backwards (as in a goofy-foot rider with his or her left foot downhill).	Someone who's always making things up.
Goofy foot	A boarder who rides with his or her right foot forwards.	Rider with feet that look like a cartoon character.
Half-pipe	A purpose-built chute with steeply banked sides, used for performing jumps.	Smoking implement broken in two.
Kicker	A ramp for jumping off.	Soccer player.
Piste	The runs in a resort that are specially prepared for boarders and skiers. They are given colours depending on how hard they are to ride.	The stuff for sticking wallpaper up with.
Planker	Skier (refers to skiers having planks on their feet).	Person who lays floorboards.
Regular foot	A boarder who rides with her or his left foot forwards.	Someone with ordinary feet.
Season	The period of time between the lifts opening at the start of winter and when they close in the spring.	Add salt and pepper.
Underground	Secret or hidden from most people; something the authorities don't like.	Where miners go.

Further Information

Information books:

There aren't very many information books aimed specifically at young people: try *Snowboarding* (Franklin Watts, 1998).

One of the most useful books for snowboarders of all ages is the *World Snowboard Guide* (Ice Publishing, first edition 1996) which is now on its third or fourth edition. It lists resorts in 57 countries and gives advice on the riding, how friendly they are to boarders, what things cost, etc.

Magazines

One of the best sources of the most recent information about snowboarding is magazines. The best UK magazines are *White Lines* (which provided the pictures from this book) and *Snowboard UK*. These are available monthly during the winter.

There are also good US-based magazines such as *Snowboarder*, although these don't tend to carry much information on the European scene.

Videos

There are a few good videos which will be listed in the magazines. However, videos to help you learn to snowboard are rare and usually not very good: the best way to learn is to go and have a couple of lessons.

The Internet

A great source of resort information (usually keying the name of the resort into the search engine will get you there): piste maps, accommodation details, transport information and so on is all available.

Most snowboard manufacturers have their own websites: again, just keying their names into a search engine usually gets you to the site.

Index

Picture Acknowlegements
All photos by Whitelines/Nick Hamilton, except page 6 (top) by Burton.